The Quiz Book for Couples

Published by Neuron Publishing
www.neuronpublishing.com
www.LoveBookOnline.com

Other LoveBook™ Titles

♡ ♡ ♡

The Original LoveBook™

A LoveBook™ is a personalized book that you create with all the reasons why you love that special someone. It s fun, easy and makes a great gift for any of your loved ones.

The Activity Book for Couples

Whether you are just dating or have been together for 50 years, these fun games and drawing activities are sure to bring laughter to your day!

The Romantic Coupon Book

A fun, romantic coupon book for anyone in love. This humorous coupon book will give your lover discounts and freebies that will keep you occupied for months! Contains 22 beautifully illustrated coupons.

The Bucket List for Couples Book

An exciting book to help couples come up with a list of goals that you'd like to achieve together. It includes categories, goal ideas, and pages to document your completed goals. A great way to spend time with your significant other while accomplishing amazing things.

The Marriage Advice Journal

This makes a great wedding or shower gift. Put all of the words of wisdom from friends and family on how to make the most of a marriage in one convenient book.

Let's Get Naked:
The Sexy Activity Book for Couples

Need to spice up your sex life? Put a little passion in your partnership? Then you need this book. It has games, quizzes, challenges and other fun stuff to get you and your partner in the mood for a little bump and tickle, if you know what I mean!

All of these titles and more can be found at
www.LoveBookOnline.com

We Do Solemnly Swear...

To play fair,
Love, laugh and learn,
Answer honestly,
and
Follow through with promised rewards.

♡ ♡ ♡

Signed:

_____

and

_____

Date:

_____

Table of Contents

ᕬ ᕬ ᕬ

Using This Book

♡ ♡ ♡

Why?

The main goal of this book is purely to have fun with your significant other and learn a little bit about one another along the way. It's a great way to spend quality time together as you try to correctly answer questions about each other and your relationship. For those of you with a competitive side, there is a place to keep score and rewards for the winner!

How?

The book is broken down into sixteen categories with questions covering everything from how well you remember your Relationship Firsts, to your partner's preferences in Entertainment and Hobbies, to your dreams for The Future and everything in between. The questions are a combination of fill in the blank, multiple choice and true/false.

To get started, decide who is going to answer the questions first. That person will be designated Person A. You can begin with whatever category you prefer. Once Person A has completed his/her answers for that category, the book gets passed to Person B who will then answer the same questions in the category on the following pages. Make sure Person B doesn't flip back to look at the answers given by Person A!

Once both people have completed the category, go back through and count how many questions each person answered correctly. Record the results on the last page of each category. The person who has the most correct answers can choose from a list of suggested rewards which will be carried out by the other person. Feel free to come up with your own rewards if you are so inspired.

Let the games begin!

Relationship Firsts

Person A: Below are some questions about all those exciting firsts in your relationship. Let´s see what you remember about those early days.

1. What would your significant other say was the most memorable part of your first date?

    _____

2. What was the first thing he/she noticed about you?
    a. a physical attribute   b. your sense of style
    c. your friendliness   d. your sense of humor

3. What was your significant other wearing on your first date?

    _____

4. Where did you go and what did you do on your first date?

    _____

    _____

5. Who made the plans for your first date?
    a. me   b. my significant other

Relationship Firsts

6. Where was your first kiss?

   _____

7. How would your significant other describe your first kiss?
   - a. short but sweet
   - b. sloppy
   - c. surprising
   - d. passionate

8. Who initiated the first time you held hands?
   - a. me
   - b. my significant other

9. What was the first holiday you spent together?

   _____

10. What was your significant other´s first impression of you?

    _____

11. How would your significant other describe the first time you met?
    - a. love at first sight
    - b. unexpected
    - c. serendipity
    - d. not in a million years

Relationship Firsts

12. What was your first song as a couple?

_____

13. What was your first major argument about?

_____

_____

14. What was the first gift that you received from your significant other?

_____

15. True/False? Your significant other was happy with the first gift you ever gave him/her.

_____

OK, it's Person B's turn! Flip the page and let's see what he/she remembers about your Relationship Firsts.

Relationship Firsts

Below are the questions that your significant other answered about the exciting firsts in your relationship. Let's see how your answers compare.

1. What would your significant other say was the most memorable part of your first date?

    _____

2. What was the first thing he/she noticed about you?
    - a. a physical attribute
    - b. your sense of style
    - c. your friendliness
    - d. your sense of humor

3. What was your significant other wearing on your first date?

    _____

4. Where did you go and what did you do on your first date?

    _____

    _____

5. Who made the plans for your first date?
    - a. me
    - b. my significant other

Relationship Firsts

6. Where was your first kiss?

   _____

7. How would your significant other describe
   your first kiss?
   - a. short but sweet
   - b. sloppy
   - c. surprising
   - d. passionate

8. Who initiated the first time you held hands?
   - a. me
   - b. my significant other

9. What was the first holiday you spent
   together?

   _____

10. What was your significant other's first
    impression of you?

    _____

11. How would your significant other describe the
    first time you met?
    - a. love at first sight
    - b. unexpected
    - c. serendipity
    - d. not in a million years

Relationship Firsts

12. What was your first song as a couple?

_____

13. What was your first major argument about?

_____

_____

14. What was the first gift that you received from your significant other?

_____

15. True/False? Your significant other was happy with the first give you ever gave him/her.

_____

That's the end of the Relationship Firsts section.
Tally your scores on the next page and see your reward!

Relationship Firsts

Quiz Results

♡ ♡ ♡

Person A: Total Number Correct ☐

Person B: Total Number Correct ☐

Rewards

♡ ♡ ♡

The person with the highest number of correct answers may choose one of the rewards below, which will be carried out by the other person. If it´s a tie, you each get to pick one.

1. Start a new tradition of your choosing with your significant other.

2. Recreate your significant other´s favorite part of your first date.

3. Take your significant other out on his/her dream date.

Hobbies

Person A: Whether it's a passion or purely for relaxation, let's find out what you know about your partner's pastimes.

1. What is your significant other's favorite thing to do in his/her free time? To do together?

    _____

2. True/False? He/She prefers participating in group sports/activities over individual sports.

    _____

3. If he/she were to invent something it would most likely be found in the...?
    a. kitchen   b. garage
    c. gym   d. latest techy magazine

4. Name an activity he/she pretends to like just because you do.

    _____

5. If he/she won a contest it would be for...?
    a. running a race   b. a beauty pageant
    c. a talent show   d. a pie eating competition

It's Person B's turn! Flip the page and give him/her a shot!

Hobbies

Person B: Take your turn and see how well you know your significant other's pastimes.

1. What is your significant other's favorite thing to do in his/her free time? To do together?

   _____

2. True/False? He/She prefers participating in group sports/activities over individual sports.

   _____

3. If he/she were to invent something it would most likely be found in the...?
   - a. kitchen
   - b. garage
   - c. gym
   - d. latest techy magazine

4. Name an activity he/she pretends to like just because you do.

   _____

5. If he/she won a contest it would be for...?
   - a. running a race
   - b. a beauty pageant
   - c. a talent show
   - d. a pie eating competition

You've completed the Hobbies section.
Tally your scores on the next page and see your reward!

Hobbies

Quiz Results

ᕲ ᕲ ᕲ

Person A: Total Number Correct ☐

Person B: Total Number Correct ☐

Rewards

ᕲ ᕲ ᕲ

The person with the highest number of correct answers may choose one of the rewards below, which will be carried out by the other person. If it's a tie, you each get to pick one.

1. Attend an activity/hobby that your significant other has always wanted you to do together.

2. Give your significant other a ´day off´ to do whatever interests him/her.

3. Challenge each other to come up with a new hobby to try together at least once a month.

Food

Person A: It's said that the way to someone's heart is through his/her stomach. How well do you know your partner's stomach?

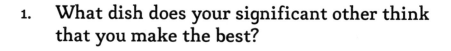

1. What dish does your significant other think that you make the best?

   _____

2. True/False? You are the better cook. _____

3. What dessert would he/she choose?
   a. ice cream   b. pie   c. cupcakes
   d. banana split   e. brownies

4. If your partner were to die tomorrow what would be his/her last meal?

   _____

5. True/False? You can usually guess what he/she is going to order at a restaurant.

   _____

6. How does your partner take his/her coffee?

   _____

It's Person B's turn! Flip the page for his/her food opinions!

❤ ❤ ❤

Food

Person B: Take your best guess at your partner's tastes with the questions below.

1. What dish does your significant other think that you make the best?

    _____

2. True/False? You are the better cook. _____

3. What dessert would he/she choose?
    a. ice cream   b. pie   c. cupcakes
    d. banana split   e. brownies

4. If your partner were to die tomorrow what would be his/her last meal?

    _____

5. True/False? You can usually guess what he/she is going to order at a restaurant.

    _____

6. How does your partner take his/her coffee?

    _____

That's the end of the Food section.
Tally your scores on the next page and see your reward!

Food

Quiz Results

♉ ♉ ♉

Person A: Total Number Correct ☐

Person B: Total Number Correct ☐

Rewards

♉ ♉ ♉

The person with the highest number of correct answers may choose one of the rewards below, which will be carried out by the other person. If it's a tie, you each get to pick one.

1. Make your significant other's favorite meal - including grocery shopping and clean-up!

2. Take your partner out to eat at his/her favorite restaurant.

3. Try one new food that your significant other loves and keep an open mind about it!

Entertainment

Person A: How familiar are you with your significant other's playlists, movie collection, reading materials and TV schedule?

1. What celebrity would your significant other want to play him/her in a movie?

   _____

2. What is his/her favorite movie genre?
    a. comedy   b. drama   c. action
    d. horror   e. romantic comedy

3. What was the last movie that you rented together?

   _____

4. How early does he/she like to get to a movie?
    a. as early as possible to get the perfect seat
    b. in time to see all the previews
    c. with enough time to get popcorn/snacks
    d. you usually end up missing the opening credits

5. True/False? He/She has made out in the back of a movie theater.

   _____

Entertainment

6. Who is your partner's all-time favorite singer?

    _____

7. What song title best describes your current
    relationship?
    - a. Ain't No Sunshine
    - b. You're Still the One
    - c. At Last
    - d. Till the End of Time

8. True/False?   You control the music when
    you're going somewhere together.

    _____

9. What song would come up as most played on
    his/her MP3 player?

    _____

10. What reading material would you most likely
    find on his/her night stand?
    - a. a latest best-seller
    - b. a romance novel
    - c. a magazine
    - d. a self-help book

11. How many books has he/she read this year?
    - a. 1 or 2   b. 3 - 7   c. 8 - 10   d. too many
    - e. you're not sure if he/she knows how to read

Entertainment

12. Where is your significant other most likely to be found reading?
    - a. in the bathroom
    - b. in bed
    - c. on a plane
    - d. on a hammock
    - e. in a waiting room

13. How does he/she prefer to read?
    - a. printed book
    - b. electronic book
    - c. audio-book
    - d. wait for the movie

14. What is his/her favorite guilty pleasure show?

    _____

15. True/False? You are more likely to share the remote for the TV.

    _____

16. You come home from vacation and realize your DVR broke. How does he/she react?
    - a. devastation - the world is over
    - b. nonchalance - it's only TV
    - c. initial panic, but saved by online TV episodes
    - d. he/she would never record TV on vacation

It's Person B's turn! Flip the page to continue the fun!

Entertainment

Person B: It's your chance to show your wealth of knowledge about your significant other's playlists, movie collection, reading materials and TV schedule.

1. What celebrity would your significant other want to play him/her in a movie?

_____

2. What is his/her favorite movie genre?
   a. comedy   b. drama   c. action
   d. horror   e. romantic comedy

3. What was the last movie that you rented together?

_____

4. How early does he/she like to get to a movie?
   a. as early as possible to get the perfect seat
   b. in time to see all the previews
   c. with enough time to get popcorn/snacks
   d. you usually end up missing the opening credits

5. True/False? He/She has made out in the back of a movie theater.

_____

Entertainment

6. Who is your partner's all-time favorite singer?

_____

7. What song title best describes your current relationship?
    a. Ain't No Sunshine   b. You're Still the One
    c. At Last   d. Till the End of Time

8. True/False? You control the music when you're going somewhere together.

_____

9. What song would come up as most played on his/her MP3 player?

_____

10. What reading material would you most likely find on his/her night stand?
    a. a latest best-seller   b. a romance novel
    c. a magazine   d. a self-help book

11. How many books has he/she read this year?
    a. 1 or 2   b. 3 - 7   c. 8 - 10   d. too many
    e. you're not sure if he/she knows how to read

Entertainment

12. Where is your significant other most likely to be found reading?
    a. in the bathroom   b. in bed   c. on a plane
    d. on a hammock   e. in a waiting room

13. How does he/she prefer to read?
    a. printed book   b. electronic book
    c. audio-book   d. wait for the movie

14. What is his/her favorite guilty pleasure show?

    _____

15. True/False? You are more likely to share the remote for the TV.

    _____

16. You come home from vacation and realize your DVR broke. How does he/she react?
    a. devastation - the world is over
    b. nonchalance - it's only TV
    c. initial panic, but saved by online TV episodes
    d. he/she would never record TV on vacation

You've completed the Entertainment section.
Tally your scores on the next page and see your reward!

♡ ♡ ♡

Entertainment

Quiz Results

ღ ღ ღ

Person A: Total Number Correct ☐

Person B: Total Number Correct ☐

Rewards

ღ ღ ღ

The person with the highest number of correct answers may choose one of the rewards below, which will be carried out by the other person. If it's a tie, you each get to pick one.

1. Take your significant other to a movie of their choice - snacks included.

2. Relinquish control of the TV remote for a week. No complaining allowed!

3. Buy tickets to see your partner's favorite band in concert.

Physical Features

Person A: Ok, the questions in this part could get you in a little bit of trouble. But don't forget you promised to answer honestly!

1. What is your significant other's favorite feature about himself/herself?

    a. hair   b. eyes   c. butt

    d. abs   e. legs   f. smile

2. What is his/her favorite feature about you?

    a. hair   b. eyes   c. butt

    d. abs   e. legs   f. smile

3. What is his/her natural hair color?

    _____

4. What body type does he/she prefer?

    a. athletic   b. average

    c. skinny   d. curvy

5. True/False? He/She is generally satisfied with his/her appearance.

    _____

Physical Features

6. If your significant other could fix one thing about his/her appearance, what would it be?

   _____

7. If your significant other could fix one thing about your appearance, what would it be?

   _____

8. True/False? Your partner has tattoos.

   _____

9. True/False? Your partner would be upset if you got a tattoo without discussing it with him/her first.

   _____

10. Which part of your partner's body is he/she least willing to show in public?
    a. feet   b. thighs   c. arms
    d. stomach   e. knees

11. Which of your physical features does he/she hope never changes?

    _____

Physical Features

12. Out of the two of you, who would your significant other say is the bigger catch?

   _____

13. Where is his/her most prominent birthmark?

   _____

14. How important are appearances to your significant other?
   a. not at all   b. only his/her own appearance
   c. very   d. important, but not everything

15. True/False? Your significant other would never get any piercings.

   _____

OK, it's Person B's turn! Flip the page and let's see what kind of trouble he/she can get into.

❤ ❤ ❤

Physical Features

Person B: You've entered some potentially dangerous territory. Do your best to match your partner's answers on looks.

1. What is your significant other's favorite feature about himself/herself?
    a. hair   b. eyes   c. butt
    d. abs   e. legs   f. smile

2. What is his/her favorite feature about you?
    a. hair   b. eyes   c. butt
    d. abs   e. legs   f. smile

3. What is his/her natural hair color?

    _____

4. What body type does he/she prefer?
    a. athletic   b. average
    c. skinny   d. curvy

5. True/False? He/She is generally satisfied with his/her appearance.

    _____

Physical Features

6. If your significant other could fix one thing about his/her appearance, what would it be?

_____

7. If your significant other could fix one thing about your appearance, what would it be?

_____

8. True/False? Your partner has tattoos.

_____

9. True/False? Your partner would be upset if you got a tattoo without discussing it with him/her first.

_____

10. Which part of your partner's body is he/she least willing to show in public?
    a. feet   b. thighs   c. arms
    d. stomach   e. knees

11. Which of your physical features does he/she hope never changes?

_____

Physical Features

12. Out of the two of you, who would your significant other say is the bigger catch?

_____

13. Where is his/her most prominent birthmark?

_____

14. How important are appearances to your significant other?
    a. not at all   b. only his/her own appearance
    c. very   d. important, but not everything

15. True/False? Your significant other would never get any piercings.

_____

You've made it through the Physical Features section. Tally your score on the next page and see your reward!

Physical Features

Quiz Results

♡ ♡ ♡

Person A: Total Number Correct ☐

Person B: Total Number Correct ☐

Rewards

♡ ♡ ♡

The person with the highest number of correct answers may choose one of the rewards below, which will be carried out by the other person. If it's a tie, you each get to pick one.

1. Tell your significant other something you like about their appearance every day for a week.

2. Help him/her accomplish a physical challenge that they've never been able to tackle alone.

3. Do something together a little outside of his/her comfort zone: dye your hair, get tattoos, pierce something, the sky is the limit!

Traits & Talents

Person A: We've covered the physical features, so now let's see how much you know about your partner on the inside.

1. Who would your significant other say is a more patient person?

    a. me   b. my significant other

2. What would he/she say is your greatest trait?

    a. optimistic   b. passionate   c. smart
    d. sensitive   e. confident   f. funny

3. What is his/her most unique, hidden talent?

    _____

4. What would he/she consider to be your most neurotic behavior?

    _____

5. Who would he/she say has the higher IQ?

    a. me   b. my significant other

Traits & Talents

6. True/False? Your significant other would describe you as outgoing.

   _____

7. What would he/she say is your greatest talent?
   a. singing   b. dancing   c. fixing
   d. cooking   e. cleaning   f. advising

8. True/False? He/She would describe you as a spiritual person.

   _____

9. What about you surprised your partner the most while he/she was getting to know you?

   _____

10. What would your partner say is his/her greatest strength?
    a. listening   b. planning   c. comforting
    d. creativity   e. good sense of direction

11. What would your partner say is his/her greatest weakness?
    a. stubbornness   b. messiness   c. quick temper
    d. forgetfulness   e. not paying attention

Traits & Talents

12. True/False? Your significant other has never stolen anything.

   _____

13. Who does your significant other do his/her best impression of?

   _____

14. What scares him/her the most?
   a. spiders   b. snakes   c. heights
   d. zombies   e. clowns   f. public speaking

15. True/False? Your significant other would offer you the window seat on a plane.

   _____

OK, it's Person B's turn! Flip the page to find out how well he/she knows your inner workings.

♡ ♡ ♡

Traits & Talents

Person B: Here are some questions that go below the surface. It's your chance to prove that you pay attention to more than what's skin deep.

1. Who would your significant other say is a more patient person?

    a. me   b. my significant other

2. What would he/she say is your greatest trait?

    a. optimistic   b. passionate   c. smart
    d. sensitive   e. confident   f. funny

3. What is his/her most unique, hidden talent?

    _____

4. What would he/she consider to be your most neurotic behavior?

    _____

5. Who would he/she say has the higher IQ?

    a. me   b. my significant other

Traits & Talents

6. True/False? Your significant other would describe you as outgoing.

   _____

7. What would he/she say is your greatest talent?
   a. singing   b. dancing   c. fixing
   d. cooking   e. cleaning   f. advising

8. True/False? He/She would describe you as a spiritual person.

   _____

9. What about you surprised your partner the most while he/she was getting to know you?

   _____

10. What would your partner say is his/her greatest strength?
    a. listening   b. planning   c. comforting
    d. creativity   e. good sense of direction

11. What would your partner say is his/her greatest weakness?
    a. stubbornness b. messiness c. quick temper
    d. forgetfulness e. not paying attention

Traits & Talents

12. True/False? Your significant other has never stolen anything.

_____

13. Who does your significant other do his/her best impression of?

_____

14. What scares him/her the most?
    a. spiders   b. snakes   c. heights
    d. zombies   e. clowns   f. public speaking

15. True/False? Your significant other would offer you the window seat on a plane.

_____

That's the end of the Traits & Talents section.
Tally your score on the next page and see your reward!

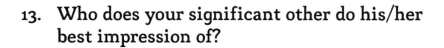

Traits & Talents

Quiz Results

♡ ♡ ♡

Person A: Total Number Correct ☐

Person B: Total Number Correct ☐

Rewards

♡ ♡ ♡

The person with the highest number of correct answers may choose one of the rewards below, which will be carried out by the other person. If it's a tie, you each get to pick one.

1. Use your best talent to do something nice for your partner. (ie. sing him/her a song)

2. Help your significant other face one of his/her fears.

3. Write a letter, card or book telling your partner how much you appreciate all the traits that make him/her so special to you.

Communication

Person A: How good are you at reading between the lines? Below are some questions to see if you've figured out what your significant other is really saying.

1. What is your first indication that your significant other is upset about something?

   _____

2. Besides you, who does he/she communicate with most often?
   - a. sibling
   - b. parent
   - c. pet
   - d. best friend
   - e. co-worker

3. What sentence or phrase do you find him/her saying the most?

   _____

4. What is the most romantic or sweetest way he/she has communicated love to you?

   _____

   _____

5. If communication in your relationship falters, who makes the first move to fix things?
   - a. me
   - b. my significant other

Communication

6. True/False? Your partner is more likely to talk about issues, rather than ignoring them.

    _____

7. Who would he/she say you talk to the most?
    a. sibling   b. parent   c. pet
    d. best friend   e. co-worker

8. True/False? He/She texts you more often than talking on the phone with you.

    _____

9. What is the most recent website you would find on his/her computer history?

    _____

10. How does he/she prefer to communicate about major issues?
    a. by phone   b. in person   c. texting
    d. email   e. carrier pigeon   d. notes

11. How many times does your partner check a social networking site per week?
    a. never   b. 1 - 5
    d. 6 - 10   e. constantly

Communication

12. Who would he/she say is better at communicating?

    a. me   b. my significant other

13. The last time your partner wrote you something by hand, what was the occasion?

    _____

14. What is the longest you've gone without communicating with each other in some way?

    a. a day   b. a week   c. a couple of hours
    d. three days e. you communicate constantly

15. True/False? Your significant other never says 'everything is fine' unless it's true.

    _____

It's Person B's turn! Flip the page and see what he/she thinks of your communication style.

♡ ♡ ♡

Communication

Person B: Let's hope you've been paying attention. These next questions are all about how you and your partner interact and get your point across.

1. What is your first indication that your significant other is upset about something?

    _____

2. Besides you, who does he/she communicate with most often?
    - a. sibling
    - b. parent
    - c. pet
    - d. best friend
    - e. co-worker

3. What sentence or phrase do you find him/her saying the most?

    _____

4. What is the most romantic or sweetest way he/she has communicated love to you?

    _____

    _____

5. If communication in your relationship falters, who makes the first move to fix things?
    - a. me
    - b. my significant other

Communication

6. True/False? Your partner is more likely to talk about issues, rather than ignoring them.

   _____

7. Who would he/she say you talk to the most?
   a. sibling   b. parent   c. pet
   d. best friend   e. co-worker

8. True/False? He/She texts you more often than talking on the phone with you.

   _____

9. What is the most recent website you would find on his/her computer history?

   _____

10. How does he/she prefer to communicate about major issues?
    a. by phone   b. in person   c. texting
    d. email   e. carrier pigeon   d. notes

11. How many times does your partner check a social networking site per week?
    a. never   b. 1 - 5
    d. 6 - 10   e. constantly

Communication

12. Who would he/she say is better at communicating?

    a. me   b. my significant other

13. The last time your partner wrote you something by hand, what was the occasion?

   _____

14. What is the longest you've gone without communicating with each other in some way?

    a. a day   b. a week   c. a couple of hours
    d. three days   e. you communicate constantly

15. True/False? Your significant other never says 'everything is fine' unless it's true.

   _____

That's it for this secation. Let's see how well you communicate. Tally your score on the next page and see your reward!

❥ ❥ ❥

Communication

Quiz Results

ᥴ ᥴ ᥴ

Person A: Total Number Correct ☐

Person B: Total Number Correct ☐

Rewards

ᥴ ᥴ ᥴ

The person with the highest number of correct answers may choose one of the rewards below, which will be carried out by the other person. If it's a tie, you each get to pick one.

1. Leave little handwritten notes for your significant other to find throughout the week.

2. Make it a point to call your partner sometime during the day, just because.

3. Sit down to dinner together, at least once a week, and have a real conversation. No phones or computers.

Intimacy

Person A: Now we're getting to the good stuff! Answer the questions below to see how connected you really are.

1. Who would your significant other say takes charge in the bedroom?

    a. me   b. my significant other

2. True/False? He/she prefers the lights on.

    _____

3. How does he/she normally sleep?

    a. stomach   b. side   c. back
    d. standing up   e. all of the above

4. What is your significant other's top fantasy?

    _____

5. How far would he/she go on a first date?

    a. hand holding   b. kissing
    c. everything but...   d. all the way

6. True/False? He/She is sexually satisfied.

    _____

It's Person B's turn! Flip the page and give him/her a shot!

♡ ♡ ♡

Intimacy

Person B: It's your turn in the hot seat. Let's see how well you do with all the intimate details.

1. Who would your significant other say takes charge in the bedroom?

    a. me   b. my significant other

2. True/False? He/she prefers the lights on.

    _____

3. How does he/she normally sleep?

    a. stomach   b. side   c. back
    d. standing up   e. all of the above

4. What is your significant other's top fantasy?

    _____

5. How far would he/she go on a first date?

    a. hand holding   b. kissing
    c. everything but...   d. all the way

6. True/False? He/She is sexually satisfied.

    _____

That's the end of the Intimacy section.
Tally your scores on the next page and see your reward!

Intimacy

Quiz Results

♥ ♥ ♥

Person A: Total Number Correct ☐

Person B: Total Number Correct ☐

Rewards

♥ ♥ ♥

The person with the highest number of correct answers may choose one of the rewards below, which will be carried out by the other person. If it's a tie, you each get to pick one.

1. Give your significant other a full body massage. One hour minimum.

2. Act out your partner's ultimate fantasy.

3. Spend an entire day together, just the two of you. No outside distractions, cell phones or computers allowed.

Travel

Person A: It could be a trip to the corner store or half-way around the world; traveling is a great test of how well you know a person.

♡?

1. Who would your significant other say is the safer driver?

    a. me   b. my significant other

2. True/False? You have a better sense of direction than him/her.

    _____

3. What would he/she prefer to do on vacation?
    a. lie in the sun   b. climb a mountain
    c. tour museums   d. visit with family

4. If you went out of town for a weekend what would he/she do while you are gone?
    a. throw a party   b. binge on junk food
    c. catch up on TV   d. mope all weekend

5. How would he/she pass the time on a road trip?
    a. sing songs   b. play games   c. sleep
    d. read   e. use his/her cell phone

It's Person B's turn! Flip the page to continue the fun.

♡ ♡ ♡

Travel

Person B: It's your turn to see how much you've picked up about your partner's travel preferences.

1. Who would your significant other say is the safer driver?

    a. me   b. my significant other

2. True/False? You have a better sense of direction than him/her.

    _____

3. What would he/she prefer to do on vacation?
    a. lie in the sun   b. climb a mountain
    c. tour museums   d. visit with family

4. If you went out of town for a weekend what would he/she do while you are gone?
    a. throw a party   b. binge on junk food
    c. catch up on TV   d. mope all weekend

5. How would he/she pass the time on a road trip?
    a. sing songs   b. play games   c. sleep
    d. read   e. use his/her cell phone

You've completed the Travel section. Tally your scores on the next page and see your reward!

Travel

Quiz Results

♡ ♡ ♡

Person A: Total Number Correct ☐

Person B: Total Number Correct ☐

Rewards

♡ ♡ ♡

The person with the highest number of correct answers may choose one of the rewards below, which will be carried out by the other person. If it's a tie, you each get to pick one.

1. Plan a trip to your significant other's dream destination. Then make it a reality.

2. Give your partner DJ rights the next time you're on a road trip.

3. Offer up the window seat (or whichever your partner prefers) the next time you're traveling.

Money

Person A: The main goal here is getting through this next section without any major arguments.

1. Who is better at handling money?

    a. me   b. my significant other

2. True/False? He/She prefers gifts from the heart rather than materialistic gifts.

    _____

3. What expense does he/she complain about?

    a. utilities   b. car repairs   c. clothes
    d. home repairs   e. entertainment   f. groceries

4. What is his/her most valued possession?

    _____

5. You win the lottery. What would he/she do?

    a. go on a luxury vacation   b. buy a fantasy car
    c. invest it   d. buy a dream home   e. donate it

6. True/False? He/She thinks it is important to keep up with the Jones's.

    _____

It's Person B's turn! Flip the page for his/her perspective.

Money

Person B: Good luck with this one. There a few land mines that you'll need to navigate.

1. Who is better at handling money?

    a. me   b. my significant other

2. True/False? He/She prefers gifts from the heart rather than materialistic gifts.

    _____

3. What expense does he/she complain about?

    a. utilities   b. car repairs   c. clothes
    d. home repairs   e. entertainment   f. groceries

4. What is his/her most valued possession?

    _____

5. You win the lottery. What would he/she do?

    a. go on a luxury vacation   b. buy a fantasy car
    c. invest it   d. buy a dream home   e. donate it

6. True/False? He/She thinks it is important to keep up with the Jones's.

    _____

That's the end of the Money section.
Tally your scores on the next page and see your reward!

Money

Quiz Results

ᑫ ᑫ ᑫ

Person A: Total Number Correct ☐

Person B: Total Number Correct ☐

Rewards

ᑫ ᑫ ᑫ

The person with the highest number of correct answers may choose one of the rewards below, which will be carried out by the other person. If it's a tie, you each get to pick one.

1. Take your significant other on a shopping spree. Determine an appropriate budget before hand.

2. Surprise your significant other with a gift. Handmade or store bought, the choice is yours.

3. Buy your significant other a lottery ticket and dream about how you'll spend the winnings.

Family

Person A: Every family has its own unique dynamic. How well do you understand your partner's family ties?

1. Who would your significant other say is closer to his/her family?

    a. me   b. my significant other

2. How would your partner describe his/her relationship with your family?

    a. wonderful   b. tolerable
    c. a struggle   d. non existent

3. Who would your significant other say is his/her favorite person in your family?

    _____

4. What is his/her favorite family tradition?

    _____

5. True/False? Your significant other would be happy living next door to his/her parents.

    _____

Family

6. Which parent would your significant other say he/she is closer to?
   - a. his/her mom
   - b. his/her dad
   - c. your mom
   - d. your dad

7. How many kids does he/she want?
   - a. none
   - b. 1 - 2
   - c. 3 - 4
   - d. not sure
   - e. enough for a sports team

8. True/False? He/She would be happy with whatever the gender of child he/she has.

   _____

9. What does the ideal family look like to your significant other?

   _____

10. What kind of baby names does he/she prefer?
    - a. traditional
    - b. modern
    - c. unique
    - d. family

11. If he/she was unable to have children naturally, what other methods would he/she consider?
    - a. adoption
    - b. IVF
    - c. surrogate
    - d. he/she would not have kids

Family

12. How would your significant other react to the news that you were having triplets?
    - a. pass out
    - b. jump for joy
    - c. get a second job
    - d. call everyone you know

13. Name something that you both agree on when it comes to raising kids.

    _____

14. How does your partner feel you should handle the holidays with both of your families?
    - a. take turns
    - b. go to both families
    - c. his/her family only
    - d. go away on vacation

15. True/False? Your partner would rather his/her parents live with you than in a nursing home.

    _____

Time to swap! Flip the page and see what Person B
really thinks about your family situation.

♋ ♋ ♋

Family

Person B: You didn't get to choose your family or your partners', but hopefully you know enough about them to get through this next set of questions.

1. Who would your significant other say is closer to his/her family?

    a. me   b. my significant other

2. How would your partner describe his/her relationship with your family?

    a. wonderful   b. tolerable
    c. a struggle   d. non existent

3. Who would your significant other say is his/her favorite person in your family?

    _____

4. What is his/her favorite family tradition?

    _____

5. True/False? Your significant other would be happy living next door to his/her parents.

    _____

Family

6. Which parent would your significant other say he/she is closer to?
    a. his/her mom
    b. his/her dad
    c. your mom
    d. your dad

7. How many kids does he/she want?
    a. none
    b. 1 - 2
    c. 3 - 4
    d. not sure
    e. enough for a sports team

8. True/False? He/She would be happy with whatever the gender of child he/she has.

    _____

9. What does the ideal family look like to your significant other?

    _____

10. What kind of baby names does he/she prefer?
    a. traditional
    b. modern
    c. unique
    d. family

11. If he/she was unable to have children naturally, what other methods would he/she consider?
    a. adoption
    b. IVF
    c. surrogate
    d. he/she would not have kids

Family

12. How would your significant other react to the news that you were having triplets?

   a. pass out   b. jump for joy
   c. get a second job d. call everyone you know

13. Name something that you both agree on when it comes to raising kids.

   _____

14. How does your partner feel you should handle the holidays with both of your families?

   a. take turns   b. go to both families
   c. his/her family only d. go away on vacation

15. True/False? Your partner would rather his/her parents live with you than in a nursing home.

   _____

That's it! Let's see how well you relate in this section.
Tally your score on the next page and see your reward!

❥ ❥ ❥

Family

Quiz Results

♡ ♡ ♡

Person A: Total Number Correct ☐

Person B: Total Number Correct ☐

Rewards

♡ ♡ ♡

The person with the highest number of correct answers may choose one of the rewards below, which will be carried out by the other person. If it's a tie, you each get to pick one.

1. Spend the next holiday with your significant other's family. No complaining.

2. Take a day off work and help your partner's family with a project or some chores.

3. Organize a family outing. Go to a sporting event, the zoo or bowling.

Pets & Animals

Person A: Love them or hate them, pets are often a part of the family. Do you know where your partner stands?

1. True/False? Your significant other has more pictures of his/her pet than of you.

   _____

2. It he/she was an animal, what would it be?

   _____

3. What is his/her stance on pets?
   a. the more the merrier   b. dogs, but no cats
   c. fine if you do the work   d. no way

4. True/False? He/She prefers the company of pets over people.

   _____

5. How would he/she react if your dog chewed his/her cell phone?
   a. shrug his/her shoulders and go buy a new one
   b. freak out - ranting, stomping and name calling
   c. gently scold the dog and clean up the mess
   d. post 'free dog' flyers around town

It's Person B's turn! Flip the page and give him/her a shot!

❣ ❣ ❣

Pets & Animals

Person B: Let's find out how you rank with the pets in your partner's life.

1. True/False? Your significant other has more pictures of his/her pet than of you.

    _____

2. If he/she was an animal, what would it be?

    _____

3. What is his/her stance on pets?
    a. the more the merrier   b. dogs, but no cats
    c. fine if you do the work   d. no way

4. True/False? He/She prefers the company of pets over people.

    _____

5. How would he/she react if your dog chewed his/her cell phone?
    a. shrug his/her shoulders and go buy a new one
    b. freak out - ranting, stomping and name calling
    c. gently scold the dog and clean up the mess
    d. post 'free dog' flyers around town

You've completed the Pets & Animals section.
Tally your scores on the next page and see your reward!

Pets & Animals

Quiz Results

❥ ❥ ❥

Person A: Total Number Correct ☐

Person B: Total Number Correct ☐

Rewards

❥ ❥ ❥

The person with the highest number of correct answers may choose one of the rewards below, which will be carried out by the other person. If it's a tie, you each get to pick one.

1. Take care of all pet-related chores for your significant other for one week.

2. Agree to pet sit your partner's animal the next time he/she is out of town.

3. Take your partner out to dinner with the money you are saving by not having a pet.

Pet Peeves

Person A: Let's see how much you know about what pushes your partner's buttons. Try not to annoy them with all of your right answers.

⌘?

1. What is your partner's all-time, biggest pet peeve?

   _____

2. What possession would he/she most like you to get rid of?

   _____

3. What would he/she say is your most irritating habit?
   a. interrupting   b. not listening   c. whining
   d. chewing with your mouth open   e. snoring

4. What trait would he/she say was cute when you first met, but now is very annoying?

   _____

5. True/False? Your partner is generally more easily annoyed than you.

   _____

It's Person B's turn! Flip the page and hand over the book.

♡ ♡ ♡

Pet Peeves

Person B: The tables are turned. How aware are you of what annoys your partner?

1. What is your partner's all-time, biggest pet peeve?

    _____

2. What possession would he/she most like you to get rid of?

    _____

3. What would he/she say is your most irritating habit?

    a. interrupting   b. not listening   c. whining
    d. chewing with your mouth open   e. snoring

4. What trait would he/she say was cute when you first met, but now is very annoying?

    _____

5. True/False? Your partner is generally more easily annoyed than you.

    _____

That's the end of the Pet Peeves section.
Tally your scores on the next page and see your reward!

Pet Peeves

Quiz Results

ᕴ ᕴ ᕴ

Person A: Total Number Correct ☐

Person B: Total Number Correct ☐

Rewards

ᕴ ᕴ ᕴ

The person with the highest number of correct answers may choose one of the rewards below, which will be carried out by the other person. If it's a tie, you each get to pick one.

1. Make a conscience effort to correct the habit that most annoys your significant other.

2. Cut your partner some slack and overlook one of the habits that you find irritating.

3. Get rid of that one piece of clothing that your significant other can't stand that you wear.

The Past

Person A: We hate to dig up the past, but if you don't know your partner's history how well do you really know them?

1. What was your significant other's greatest fear as a child?

   _____

2. What did he/she want to be as a grown up?
   a. ballerina   b. fireman   c. president
   d. doctor   e. teacher   f. famous

3. Who was his/her best friend as a child?

   _____

4. What was his/her first pet?

   _____

5. True/False? Your significant other looks back on his/her childhood fondly.

   _____

The Past

6. How many boyfriends/girlfriends did he/she have before you?
   a. less than 3   b. 3 - 4
   c. 5 - 6   d. more than you can count

7. How old was your partner on his/her first date?
   a. a baby   b. 14 - 16
   c. 17 - 18   d. a late bloomer

8. True/False? He/She had a good relationship with his/her siblings.

   _____

9. Who would your significant other say had the greatest influence on his/her life?

   _____

10. What type of student was he/she?
    a. straight ´A´s   b. barely passed
    c. average   d. involved in everything

11. What was his/her favorite activity as a kid?
    a. sports   b. camp   c. scouts
    d. drawing   e. swimming   f. bike riding

The Past

12. True/False? Your partner was on the homecoming/prom court in high school.

_____

13. Where did your significant other go to college?

_____

14. What other area of interests did he/she have outside of his/her chosen career path?
    a. health   b. technology
    c. arts   d. communication

15. True/False? If your significant other could do it all over again he/she would have pursued a different career.

_____

OK, it's Person B's turn! Flip the page and find out how much he/she has uncovered about your past.

❣ ❣ ❣

The Past

Person B: Assuming you didn't grow up together, it's time to find out how nosy you were when getting to know your significant other.

1. What was your significant other's greatest fear as a child?

_____

2. What did he/she want to be as a grown up?
   a. ballerina   b. fireman   c. president
   d. doctor   e. teacher   f. famous

3. Who was his/her best friend as a child?

_____

4. What was his/her first pet?

_____

5. True/False? Your significant other looks back on his/her childhood fondly.

_____

The Past

6. How many boyfriends/girlfriends did he/she have before you?
   a. less than 3   b. 3 - 4
   c. 5 - 6   d. more than you can count

7. How old was your partner on his/her first date?
   a. a baby   b. 14 - 16
   c. 17 - 18   d. a late bloomer

8. True/False? He/She had a good relationship with his/her siblings.

   _____

9. Who would your significant other say had the greatest influence on his/her life?

   _____

10. What type of student was he/she?
    a. straight ´A´s   b. barely passed
    c. average   d. involved in everything

11. What was his/her favorite activity as a kid?
    a. sports   b. camp   c. scouts
    d. drawing   e. swimming   f. bike riding

The Past

12. True/False? Your partner was on the homecoming/prom court in high school.

_____

13. Where did your significant other go to college?

_____

14. What other area of interests did he/she have outside of his/her chosen career path?
    a. health   b. technology
    c. arts   d. communication

15. True/False? If your significant other could do it all over again he/she would have pursued a different career.

_____

That's the end of your look into each other's past.
Tally your score on the next page and see your reward!

♡ ♡ ♡

The Past

Quiz Results

♡ ♡ ♡

Person A: Total Number Correct ☐

Person B: Total Number Correct ☐

Rewards

♡ ♡ ♡

The person with the highest number of correct answers may choose one of the rewards below, which will be carried out by the other person. If it's a tie, you each get to pick one.

1. Take your significant other to a place that is nostalgic for him/her.

2. Plan a movie night and rent your partner's favorite movie growing up.

3. Listen to your partner share some of his/her favorite memories from his/her past.

The Future

Person A: Now that we've uncovered the past, it only makes sense to see how much the two of you have discussed about your future.

♡?

1. Does your significant other prefer to plan ahead or take things as they come?

   a. planner   b. come what may

2. Where does he/she want to retire?

   a. on a RV   b. where the grandkids are

   c. by the beach   d. traveling the world

3. Which ability would be the hardest for him/her to lose in old age?

   a. sight   b. smell   c. hearing

   d. mobility   e. chewing

4. What is his/her greatest lifelong dream?

   _____

5. What part of old-age is he/she most looking forward to?

   a. grandkids   b. senior discounts

   c. traveling   d. retirement

It's Person B's turn! Flip the page for his/her take on the future!

♡ ♡ ♡

The Future

Person B: Don't worry, you won't be asked to predict your future. Just try to match your partner's vision of things to come.

1. Does your significant other prefer to plan ahead or take things as they come?

    a. planner   b. come what may

2. Where does he/she want to retire?

    a. on a RV   b. where the grandkids are
    c. by the beach   d. traveling the world

3. Which ability would be the hardest for him/her to lose in old age?

    a. sight   b. smell   c. hearing
    d. mobility   e. chewing

4. What is his/her greatest lifelong dream?

    _____

5. What part of old-age is he/she most looking forward to?

    a. grandkids   b. senior discounts
    c. traveling   d. retirement

That's the end of this one. Tally your scores on the next page.

The Future

Quiz Results

♥ ♥ ♥

Person A: Total Number Correct ☐

Person B: Total Number Correct ☐

Rewards

♥ ♥ ♥

The person with the highest number of correct answers may choose one of the rewards below, which will be carried out by the other person. If it's a tie, you each get to pick one.

1. Make a bucket list of things that you and your partner want to accomplish in the future.

2. Help your significant other plan and achieve one of his/her future goals.

3. Sign up for a class that has always interested your partner and take it together.

General

Person A: You've made it to the catch-all section with all those great off-the-wall questions. It's your last chance to prove that you're the most knowledgeable.

1. Who takes longer to get ready in the morning?
   a. me   b. my significant other

2. What magical power would your partner choose to have?
   a. mind control   b. invisibility
   c. telepathy   d. healing

3. What is his/her favorite holiday?

   _____

4. What is his/her astrological sign?

   _____

5. If the house was on fire and your significant other could grab one thing, what would it be?

   _____

General

6. What cartoon character does your significant other relate to the most?

   _____

7. If he/she was stuck on a desert island and could only bring one thing, what would it be?
   a. liquor   b. matches   c. sunscreen
   c. favorite book   d. MP3 player

8. What smell reminds your partner of you?

   _____

9. What sound reminds your partner of you?

   _____

10. What is his/her favorite color to wear?

    _____

11. How many hours of sleep does your partner need to feel his/her best?
    a. 4 - 5 maximum   b. can get by on 6 - 7
    c. solid 8 hours   d. 9 +, minimum

General

12. True/False?   If your partner was a superhero, he/she would use the power for good.

_____

13. What celebrity would he/she leave you for?

_____

14. If you wanted to ask him/her for a big favor, when is the best time to ask?
    a. first thing in the morning   b. after coffee
    c. just before bed   d. after a workout

15. True/False?   Your significant other squeezes the toothpaste from the middle of the tube.

_____

Time to give person B a shot! Flip the page and see how much random information he/she knows about you.

♡ ♡ ♡

General

Person B: Get ready for the fun questions and your last chance to prove that you really know your stuff!

1. Who takes longer to get ready in the morning?
    a. me   b. my significant other

2. What magical power would your partner choose to have?
    a. mind control   b. invisibility
    c. telepathy   d. healing

3. What is his/her favorite holiday?

    _____

4. What is his/her astrological sign?

    _____

5. If the house was on fire and your significant other could grab one thing, what would it be?

    _____

General

6. What cartoon character does your significant other relate to the most?

7. If he/she was stuck on a desert island and could only bring one thing, what would it be?
   a. liquor   b. matches   c. sunscreen
   c. favorite book   d. MP3 player

8. What smell reminds your partner of you?

9. What sound reminds your partner of you?

10. What is his/her favorite color to wear?

11. How many hours of sleep does your partner need to feel his/her best?
    a. 4 - 5 maximum   b. can get by on 6 - 7
    c. solid 8 hours   d. 9 +, minimum

General

12. True/False? If your partner was a superhero, he/she would use the power for good.

_____

13. What celebrity would he/she leave you for?

_____

14. If you wanted to ask him/her for a big favor, when is the best time to ask?
    a. first thing in the morning   b. after coffee
    c. just before bed   d. after a workout

15. True/False? Your significant other squeezes the toothpaste from the middle of the tube.

_____

That's it! That's all she wrote. You know the drill.
Tally your scores on the next page and see your reward!

♥ ♥ ♥

General

Quiz Results

♡ ♡ ♡

Person A: Total Number Correct ☐

Person B: Total Number Correct ☐

Rewards

♡ ♡ ♡

The person with the highest number of correct answers may choose one of the rewards below, which will be carried out by the other person. If it's a tie, you each get to pick one.

1. Take your significant other out for his/her favorite dessert.

2. Clean your partner's car - inside and out!

3. Take your partner on a day trip of his/her choice (ie. day at the beach, golfing, spa, whale watching...you get the picture.)

Final Results

Congratulations! You've completed all of the questions, hopefully had a few laughs and learned a little more about each other along the way. For those of you with the drive to compete, there's only one thing left to do. Tally all of your correct questions throughout the book and record them below to determine the overall winner!

Person A: Total Number Correct ☐

Person B: Total Number Correct ☐

Reward

♡ ♡ ♡

You clearly know your significant other well and have earned some much deserved bragging rights. What greater reward is there than quality time spent together? Bask in your glory, enjoy each other's company and learn something new about each other every day!

About LoveBook™

We are a group of individuals who want to spread love in all its forms. We believe love fuels the world and every relationship is important. We hope this book helps build on that belief.